To my mother, Be_____r Artists for openly sharin_____ _____ and experiences in a diverse and welcoming online community; and to Ashley, Chyann, Jill, and all my other amazing friends who have supported me throughout this adventure.

Contents

Foreword

Chapter 1: Tools of the Trade

Chapter 2: Mixing Your Palette

Chapter 3 Layering Your Cup

Chapter 4: Time to Pour

Chapter 5: Finishing Work

Chapter 6: Taking It To The Next Level

About the Author

Foreword

Welcome to the eclectic world of Flow Painting, also known as Fluid Painting and Acrylic Pouring! Flow Painting can be a therapeutic and rewarding form of art for almost anyone from any background. If you enjoy crafts and DIY projects but have never formally studied Color Theory, Drawing, or Design, don't worry - you CAN do this! Fluid art is mesmerizing to watch and endlessly entertaining to experiment with, but it can also look deceptively simple to execute. Getting started requires a thorough knowledge of the steps, techniques, and tools involved, but the educational resources and opinions are seemingly endless! This beginner's guide will take you through not only the basics you need to to get started, but all the major points of interest as you advance with your skills and consistency - all while helping you to avoid common pitfalls. We'll cover the tools you'll need, basic layering and pouring techniques, and even how to create a professional brand around your Artwork. Everything that follows comes from my own practice, experiments, and personal experiences. Those are based not only on developing my own body of work, but also from teaching Flow Painting Classes and developing my own unique professional quality line of Primal Flow Pre-Mixed Acrylic Pouring Paints. What I've included here is based on what I've found that works for my students and I, regardless of their level of experience or artistic background. One of the most interesting features of Acrylic Pouring is how many ways it can be done – the possibilities are literally endless! Every artist has their own preferred supplies, tools, and techniques - this book barely scratches the surface - but I believe this detailed overview will give you a solid foundation on which to build your skills. We all have to start somewhere, but my hope is that reading this will get you started on the best foot possible!

-*Kegan Kidd, Primal Flow Studio*

Chapter 1:
Tools of the Trade

You've probably seen the mesmerizing flow painting videos and the beautiful artwork created by friends and family and you're ready to give it a shot! Admittedly, the most intimidating part of starting out in acrylic pour painting is figuring out what tools and techniques you need to get started. The two things that every beginner should be ready for is that you may not produce 'successful' work at first, and that practicing paint mixing and pouring techniques with the wrong materials can become very expensive very quickly. Not everyone has the same financial ability to start with high end products, so this guide is geared towards keeping things simple, functional, and affordable! You also need to consider your space allowance before you begin shopping. Take into consideration not only how much space you have to actually work, but also how much you have to allow pieces to dry without being touched/moved. You don't want to buy gallons of paint and flow medium to start when you only have room to do a few small pieces every few days. Please note there is a Glossary in the back of this book for any unfamiliar words/terms.

1) Canvases

First and foremost, I always suggest starting with smaller work while you are still getting comfortable with the process as well as learning consistency in your techniques. For example, my students use 8" x 10" canvases in their first few classes as the largest piece they work on. Smaller canvases are easy to handle, display well when finished, and are fairly affordable in bulk. I would suggest staying away from flat canvas boards, as they will curve on you as they dry and typically don't look professional unless they are framed (which can be costly). I would also leave more difficult items (like wood, tiles, 3D shapes, phone cases, trays, etc.) for a alter time when you feel really comfortable in your pour techniques. Remember – there is a learning curve with any artistic technique! You will like your results so much more over time if you have a little patience and put in the practice!

2) Clear Plastic Cups & Plastic Knives/Spoons

This is a must-have for me, and I frequently buy these in bulk to keep costs down. Clear plastic cups and boxes of plastic picnic cutlery are easy to find, easy to use, and easily washable. I prefer smaller cups to start out because it is very easy to mix and layer too much paint for any particular piece. I also suggest starting with 4-6oz cups, and then moving on to larger 8-12oz cups when you want to start working larger. Clear cups are preferable, as they can help dramatically with layering your paints and gauging the amount you're using.

3) Plastic Storage Tubs

These are undeniably the most mess-free tool to use in acrylic pour painting and resin work. Short 4-6" tall tubs that are at least 2 feet long will catch your drips and protect the surrounding surfaces from unwanted drops and spills. You can prop your work on overturned cups or small wire racks. You should always avoid setting wet artwork on a solid surface, as your piece could end up glued to it by dried paint. It also doesn't allow air underneath for even drying. If you experiment with Resin work later on, I highly suggest large tubs with lids to place your pieces in to dry so that no dust, bugs, or flecks can settle into them. Resin hardens by chemical reaction and not via air flow, so please note that I do not recommend enclosed tubs for drying acrylic flow painted pieces. Some artists use tubs to slow drying on larger acrylic pieces and avoid crazing, but I find that perfecting the technique of a thinner, even pour with good air flow above and below as it dries works just as well with low risk. If you don't have a cool, dust-free area to work however, enclosing your drying works in level, enclosed tubs is an viable option.

***Stay SAFE! Remember to always work in a well ventilated area! I cannot stress this enough – if you are mixing, pouring, finishing/glossing, or even if you have a lot of works stored and curing – the space should be well ventilated for your safety. Some fumes aren't even noticeable until they've already done damage to your throat and lungs.

4) Level (Or Level App)

Even having a small level on hand can make a BIG difference in your pieces. Whatever shelves or cups you set out to dry your pieces on need to be completely level - even the smallest tilt to one side or corner can allow the paint to slide off and ruin your piece while it settles and dries. Take a clean ruler or stiff piece of cardboard and lay it down on the farthest edge of your drying rack or cups. Place your level on top, and repeat this around each side, adjusting as needed until all four sides (and the center) read level. I personally like sheets of thick cardstock printing paper that I can fold to different thicknesses to make small adjustments under wire racks and small tubs. I also use 1" and 4" square ceramic tiles to make larger adjustments under larger tubs.

5)Latex Gloves

These are great for keeping your hands covered and clean. Not always the best option given the cost, but the food grade gloves tend to be more affordable than the medical grade. Unfortunately the food grade can fit looser and can get in the way more than they help. If you have sensitive skin or nails to protect, this is the way to go, but expect to change them frequently so that you aren't transferring wet paint from or your cups to your tools, work surfaces, or other piece of art.

6) Paper Towels/Rags

I warn my students from the outset that it is nearly impossible to have fun flow painting and manage to stay clean. I find wiping off my hands between steps is easier than wearing and changing gloves constantly. I'm a fan of finding tattered and thinning towels, hand rags, and t-shirts to cut into squares to use as hand and cup wipes. Afterwards, I either drop them into a bucket of water to wash out and reuse or just throw them away. Paper towels or tough shop towels and rags are also good options.

7) Paint

Rainbow Pack of Pre-Mixed Primal Flow Acrylic Pouring Paints

Mixing your own colors can be a lot of fun, but it can also be an obstacle, as learning how to get the right consistency and opacity without dulling your colors is tough! Take the stress out of learning how to flow paint by starting with pre-mixed and ready-to-pour colors. My own line of Primal Flow Paints are vivid, have a unique creamy consistency, and are totally safe and water based for easy clean up. Starting with a ready-made paint lets you focus on gaining confidence and technique, but also cuts down on costs and your prep time dramatically. Once you branch out into mixing your own colors, you can utilize Primal Flow Paints as an addition to your pour to add shimmer and depth to your work. We will discuss mixing your own colors from scratch in a later chapter.

I always advise shaking or stirring all your paint right before use, as well as double-checking them for lumps. When mixed with your flow medium, your paint should have very little resistance when stirred and drip easily from the point of your stirring utensil. If it looks and feels syrupy, it may need more flow medium. Getting a good handle on getting an even consistency in the beginning is one of the the building blocks for learning to vary consistency as a technique later on.

8) Flow Medium (Pouring/Fluid/Flow Medium, Flow Aid, etc.)

There are a lot of options at a lot of different price points, which means there is plenty of room to experiment! Some brands like Liquitex are very smooth but very expensive. Others like Flood Floetrol are very affordable, but it does add a bit of texture to a piece (and may have to be strained before use). Primal Flow Medium has a sparkly, secret ingredient that actually boosts cells and lacing - it is completely unique in the medium market! Once you get comfortable, a second step can be taken by experimenting with changing the consistencies of your colors to be a little different from one another - some thinner, some thicker. This changes the way the colors will interact and settle. I would advise against using water as an additive to any of your paints while you are learning, as it can cause issues like the colors over-mixing and become 'muddy.' It can also cause some issues like crazing and cracking as your pieces dry due to less flexibility and broken down acrylic bonds between the pigments – especially since and your pieces might be a bit thicker in the beginning.

9) Torch

This one can be intimidating, but take it into consideration as you prepare. This is a tool that isn't totally necessary from the outset for a beginner, but does have some merits. The trick to torching is to NOT touch the paint with the flame, but rather move it smoothly and somewhat quickly back and forth over the surface, popping bubbles with the hot air expelled by the flame (which also creates and expands cells). This helps avoid the small pitmarks that form as bubbles pop by themselves after the paint has partially set and stiffened. Bubbles tend to come to the top over several minutes, and the thicker your pour is, the longer that process takes. I usually suggest torching when you set the piece down to dry, and then again 5-10 minutes later to catch any late rising bubbles. It also tends to open cells if you use any sort of oil or dry pigment additive in your pour, as the torch heats the oils, which then expand. You can also pop bubbles with your breath or by gently running a hair dryer over the surface, but very carefully so as not to move the paint around. If you are interested in adding a torch to your toolbox, I highly suggest small culinary torches that are refillable with butane (available wherever lighters are sold). Always keep them safely away from children and flammable items and paints. For safety, I store my paints, torch and butane refills separately.

10) Sandpaper

I always recommend having this on hand - preferably a very fine 220 grit - available at any hardware store. I also prefer the smaller, tear-away sheets that fit easily in your hand. Sandpaper is primarily used during the finishing work, after your pieces have dried. It is also handy if you want to reuse a canvas, as it is advisable to sand it back down smooth so the texture from the previous pour doesn't show through the new one. If you want to work on anything wood, I suggest you also get a slightly larger grit as well. When you prep a wooden piece to pour on, first lightly sand (with the grain) with the larger grit paper, then sand again with the finer grit. This will get it the smoothest surface with the least friction. Wipe off the fine dust with a damp sponge or rag and allow it to dry before the next step.

11) Finishing Gloss

You'll notice as your pieces dries that they will likely go dull and lose most of their vibrancy. Not to worry – a little finishing work will bring it back to life! If you choose to go with a spray, you want to choose something glossy but durable. There are a lot of possibilities, from lower-end Rustoleum gloss sprays to high-end options by brands like Winsor-Newton. I always suggest experimenting with the lower-end varieties as you practice on earlier pieces, then move on to the higher-end varieties as you gain experience and confidence in your work. I personally use a heat-resistant gloss enamel that is meant for automotive use. I would advise staying away from liquid gloss glazes, resins, and polyurethane at first, as they all need a lot of technical experience to use successfully.

Prepping Your Work Space

When you set up your work area, make sure everything you need is easily within reach. You will also need a dust and bug free area prepared for drying pieces to rest without being moved, bumped into, or dripped and splattered on. I use a small green house that is essentially a small rolling shelving unit with 4 wire shelves and a plastic cover. It works perfectly as a slow-drying rack for pieces up to 11" x 14", after they've been sitting at least 6 hours are no longer in danger of dripping. If you're using a solid surface like tables or shelves, upturned plastic cups put under each corner (under the wood, not the canvas itself) are an easy and reusable way to set up canvases for drying.

Chapter 2: Mixing Your Palette

The first and best tip for mixing colors is this: if you're mixing your own paints, stay away from the cheapest brands! Brands like Apple Barrel and Liquitex 'Basics' have a low pigment density, which can translate to a lot of unwanted blending and potentially muddy colors. When I look through Instagram for example, I can almost always spot pieces that were made with Liquitex Basics because they look dull in pours to me, even when glossed. Let me break down why pigment density is important:

Imagine a tube of paint is an 8oz glass of Sweet Tea, and the Color Pigments in it are the granules of sugar. Cheap acrylic paints would only have 1 teaspoon of sugar per glass of tea, whereas high end colors have 3+ tablespoons of sugar in the same size glass. Imagine drinking both of those – you would definitely be able to taste the difference. Adding Flow Medium to your paint is like adding more Unsweet Tea to those glasses of Sweet Tea. The sugar will re-distribute throughout the new mix, becoming diluted. In the first glass, you may not even be able to taste the sugar anymore, but in the second glass you would just have slightly-less-sweet Sweet Tea. Because we add that medium to the mix, diluting those pigments, the paint we start with really matters! All of this is to say that I suggest starting with middle of the road brands from a hobby art store instead of the Tempera or Acrylics paints from your local big box retailer.

When you start mixing your colors up, start with a 1 to 1 ratio of paint and flow medium; i.e. about 1 inch of paint in your cup and then 1 inch of medium on top of that, then mix thoroughly. If you feel like the color is still too thick, go to a 2 to 1 ratio – you want it less like syrup, more like whole milk. Getting the right consistency can be very subjective, but if you start out aiming for the same consistency in each color, you'll naturally develop a feel for how much medium you need/want. The number one issue with new artists is leaving their paints too thick in the beginning! Every paint will have a different consistency and transparency starting out – even if they're all from the same brand. Some paints are just going to need more medium than others to get where you want them.

Color Theory – What Works Together and What Doesn't

When it comes to your color choices, the best advice I can give is start with your favorite color, and then begin matching colors to it monochromatically instead of complementary. In layman's terms, try to keep to colors that are similar instead of opposing color pairs like Purple/Yellow, Blue/Orange, and Green/Red. Those complementary colors are much more likely to become brown 'mud' if they over-mix. For example, if you want to start with Blue, start with a Monochromatic palette but vary your tones, i.e. Baby Blue, Navy Blue, Cerulean (like a dark blue/green), light Turquoise Blue, and White. This way, you have dark colors AND light colors for contrast, but if they do over-blend they will still look good together and not become brown or flat looking. Again, this is just when you are starting out - you'll naturally gain confidence and begin to vary your color choices and find what speaks to you.

When it comes to how many colors per pour to use, starting simple is more advisable than getting too 'busy' too quickly. Dramatic pours with 10+ color pours can certainly look amazing, but I promise it took those artists <u>a lot</u> of practice and patience to make that technique work successfully. Start out with 3-6 colors per pour and give yourself time to work your way up to those alluring rainbow-esque pours. When I set up to work, I will often mix up a set palette of 6 to 8 colors and do several pieces in just that palette, while varying my layering and pouring techniques with each piece. I may do 6-10 pieces in a sitting that all have the same colors, but they will still look dramatically different from one-another thanks to those variations. One of the most freeing things about pour painting is that no matter how much you prepare, you absolutely cannot guarantee what the finished product will look like. The key is to be adaptable and make instinctive choices on how to pour/tilt/stretch your piece in the moment. You can layer two cups identically, use the same pour on both on two identical surfaces, and still get completely different pieces! Keeping the palette simple in the beginning is in no way limiting what your final product can will be!

Chapter 3: Layering Your Cup

When preparing for acrylic pouring, how you layer each color in your cup might be the most important part of this entire process, but it can also be the most deceptively simple. To help you understand the importance of thoughtful layering, I have 3 suggested techniques for you to try out. Using the same 3-6 colors throughout can also help you see how different layering

techniques affect how each each finished piece will look.

Example of Cup Layering Technique #1

Cup 1: Very gently pour about a quarter inch of your darkest (or favorite) color into the bottom of your cup. When you pour the second color, gently tilt your cup and pour the paint down the inside of the cup, allowing it to pool over the first color - again approximately 1/4" thick. Repeat this process, stacking your colors light/dark/light (for contrast) until your cup is full enough for your canvas size. Example: for a 9oz cup and a 8 x 10 canvas, this would be about 3/4 full for a beginner. You'll quickly discover on your pours whether you have too much or not enough paint – play it by ear based on the size of the pieces you are working on. This will give you cleaner, bolder colors that mix less.

Cup 2: Again, start with a 1/4" of your darkest (or favorite) color first, the pour the second color directly into the center of the cup. Repeat with all your colors, letting the gravity of the pour carry them down through the center of the mix. They will often sink through - sometimes fully out of sight - and that is okay! Repeat until the cup is full enough to pour. This will give you a more blended look in your final piece.

Cup 3: This one is a little more time consuming, but absolutely worth learning. Start again with the same first color as before. Using your stirring utensil (a plastic spoon works best), gently drizzle each of your chosen colors into the cup, one by one. You'll be able to see the previous colors layered below, with a little swirl of the newest color on top. On some colors, you can do heavier drizzles until it nearly covers the top completely. Keep going, alternating colors until your cup is ready. This one is usually a lot of fun, with lots of pop of vibrancy, some cool shading, and if you're lucky, some really nice, oft lacing. Lacing is one of my favorite visual results - think seafoam on the beach as the ocean recedes. Absolutely beautiful, but very sensitive to over-stretching (discussed in the next chapter.) Some other tips that you may find helpful as you progress are as follows:

- If you use an oil additive, try adding it to only half your colors, and then layer those colors every other layer (i.e. oil, no oil, oil, etc.) This maximizes the reaction between your oil additive and the water content in the paints that do not have oil, resulting in really nice cells!

- Remember that the bottom color will most likely end up being the most visible, depending on your pour technique. For example, if you're going for a bright piece with subtle dark contrast, start your layering with a bright color, not a dark one.

— If you are going to vary the consistencies in your colors, trying layering your cups from the thickest to thinnest paint. There is a lot of chemistry that happens between thinner paints and thicker paints, so play with this technique, but try to have a plan going in!

Chapter 4: Time to Pour!

Before tackling your very first pour, there are three things you should try to keep in mind:

1) This style of painting is NOT about control or perfection. It's about color, movement, and letting your art form organically. You will never be able to get the exact same result twice, and that's okay! The most therapeutic part of this for so many people is realizing they just have to let go and let themselves enjoy the process. Going for consistency is great, but enjoying the journey is just as important!

2) You may not like everything you make, and that is perfectly normal! There is no shame in scraping wet paint off a canvas and trying again. The main difference between a hobbyist and an Artist is that a hobbyist will love everything they make (and often try to sell every single thing, regardless of how successful it is.) An Artist takes that emotional attachment at least partially out of the equation and focuses on mastering the techniques that consistently create the most successful pieces. For example, if you create 10 pieces and feel that only 1

of them in successful, you are gaining a more critical professional eye for your own work. Keep learning, refining, and evolving!

3) You don't have to have a Bachelor Degree in Arts, have mastered color theory, or have ever studied fine art in any way, shape, or form. I believe every child has an innate artistic inclination that is slowly starved for want of use. Every human being alive has a primal part of their brain that appreciates certain colors and shapes and pleasing organic structures. It's rare to find a person who isn't moved by gently rolling waves on a beach, the colorful structure of a geode, or the wispy, gaseous formations of distant galaxies. The best advice I can give it to start with what moves you and go from there. What is your favorite color? What colors do you best like together in your home decor? What forms in nature inspire you? Finding a place to start really can be as simple as taking your inspiration from a throw pillow or spray of flowers or a pretty rock in your window.

Tricks of the Trade: Dry Priming vs. Wet Priming

Beginners often ask if they should prime/gesso their canvases before they start painting. There are some basic guidelines (and wildly varying opinions) for gessoing, but no set rules where it concerns acrylic pouring. Most canvases these days are pre-primed, but gessoing can make them even smoother to work on, as canvas has a very recognizable texture. Many artists gesso with flat house paint, which I personally find to be the most affordable option. When you work on wood products, they soak up a lot of the moisture from the paint, sometimes causing cracking and crazing. I prefer to wet-prime my canvases (discussed below) and dry prime my wood pieces with a light layer of paint or wood sealant. This is done to cut down on how much water they absorb, as that can also cause bowing/curving in thinner wood pieces. If you want to rework a piece you've done but don't like, do your best to scrape it off while it's wet, or you'll need to sand it down when it has dried completely. In some cases, you may need to thoroughly sand, re-gesso, and allow them to dry fully before reworking them. You can also sand them down and spray a layer of the same glossing agent you use to finish pieces as an easy sealant.

What is Wet Priming?

The biggest issue to getting clean lines and cells in a pour is finding a way around the friction caused by the dry surface – even on one that has been primed. That friction keeps the paint from moving easily over the surface, which means you may have to 'stretch' the paint more than you really should just to get the paint over all the edges and corners. The best way to get around this is to have a 'base' color mixed up and prepared that is purely to aid in resolving friction. For beginners I suggest a basic white paint (partly because it's nearly always a nice color addition for pours) mixed 1 part paint to 2 parts flow medium. Immediately before you start layering your cup, take your base color, pour a little on the outside edges of your canvas surface and spread it around gently (with a tool or your hands.) Be sure to cover every single dry spot of canvas (especially edges and corners!) The trick is to keep it fairly thin; if you think it's too thickly applied (showing texture & lines), pick up and tilt the canvas to pour the excess off the edges. You can also pour it directly in the center and tilt to cover your canvas as you would with a pour. This is great practice for tilting your later work (as well as looking for bald spots.) The paint from your actual pours will push this base paint off or glide right over it - as long as you've just done it and it doesn't have time to set/start to dry. This greatly reduces friction, giving you a much cleaner and smoother look. This also helps with moving the paint from your actual pour in as few directions as possible after it's on your canvas. Allowing it to glide smoothly also means you can keep your own arm movements fluid and avoid those messy looking peaks and swirls so often seen on over-worked, over-stretched flow paintings. The base color shouldn't show through unless you leave some negative space or stretch your work a little too thin, allowing it to rise and create cells. We'll discuss the merits of negative space a little later on.

Adding Oil

After you've mastered the basics, you will probably want to experiment with adding oil to your pours to create big, beautiful 'cells'! Two of the most popular choices for an oil additive are Treadmill Oil and Blaster Silicone. Do some research on what to experiment with, but know that everyone may recommend something different! I personally use Blaster Silicone, as it's easy to get and a bottle will last me a year or more. It just takes a tiny squirt per cup to achieve the desired result. For bigger cells, you can also add oil to half your colors and a few drops of water to the other colors. This is another element that trial and error will be the best way to work out how much, how often, and whether it creates an effect you like.

Adding oil can have some downsides! It may slow the drying time of your work considerably, and make your paint more likely to slide over the edges while your work is setting/drying. It also means you'll need to clean/de-oil your paint surface before it can be finished/glossed. I recommended using a soft rag to gently wipe down your artwork with 75% Alcohol after it is completely dry. Don't wipe any area more than once, and allow it to dry fully before handling again. If you see any shiny spots, gently repeat the process. This is especially important if you are going to Resin coat!

Basic Pour Techniques for Beginners:

These are the tried-and true basic pours that every fluid artist – beginner to professional – should strive to master. Consistency is key, and it all starts with your mixing, layering, and pouring techniques.

1)The Tried and True Flip Cup

This may be the first pour for any beginner, but trust me - anyone who regularly flow paints comes back to this one again and again! If you have your canvas wet primed and your cup layered, you're ready to go.

Part 1: Pick up your canvas (as much from underneath as possible so your hands don't take the wet paint off any more of the edge than necessary.) Pick up your cup in the other hand (but be careful not to squeeze). This part will take some practice, but in one smooth motion, quickly turn the canvas almost fully upside down, and then lift your cup and set the canvas on top of it, as centered as possible. With the canvas is now laying on top of the cup, move your canvas-holding hand to the underside of the canvas itself – palm flat against where the cup is. Maintain pressure from both sides as you flip the canvas back over, keeping the cup firmly attached (and the paint trapped inside until you're ready, but do NOT squeeze your cup!) Once you're holding the canvas flat again with the cup upside down on top of it, you can gently let go of the cup (which should stick due to suction). With both hands on either end, very gently set the canvas back down flat on your work surface.

Part 2: Position your cup in the center (if needed) by very gently dragging (as you gently push down to maintain suction). Tap the top of your cup a few times to encourage all the paint to pool at the bottom (which helps avoid drips) and wait a few moments for everything to slide down. With one hand, gently squeeze the cup as you lift it just a fraction of an inch. The paint should slowly pool out from under the cup, sometimes with little 'gasps' as the cup pulls in air to replace the paint in the vacuum that is still formed. Slowly lift the cup until that seal is broken (the remaining paint will quickly pool out.) Quickly pull the cup up, away, and to the side so that the paint dripping from the inside edges doesn't drip into the pool of paint now on the canvas. What you should have is a bubble of paint with a circular design towards the top that will quickly begin to settle and spread.

The second technique that is sometimes employed here is to use a sharp tool to quickly pierce the underside of your cup as you hold it down on the canvas. This breaks the seal formed inside the cup, and the paint will pool out very quickly when you lift it. Both styles have their pros and cons, so try each and see which feels more comfortable for you.

Part 3: Time to 'stretch' your work! The name of the game is to strike a balance here between covering the entire canvas, keeping the final product from being so thick that it continues to slide off the edges after you're done, and not overworking it (losing all your cells and lacing that should be forming as it settles.) This will take a lot of practice, so don't get discouraged if it doesn't go perfectly the first time or two. Gently pick your piece up from underneath on 2 corners, avoiding touching the outside edges. Slowly tilt it toward the farthest right corner. In the beginning, the slower you tilt the better! If you let the paint move too fast, it will stretch too much AND lose too much paint over the side before you have the canvas fully covered.

The **Corner-Dip** technique (also called the Dip-And-Snap) may be necessary to totally cover your corners. As you tilt towards a corner, the paint can sometimes simply go around it (like water around a boulder in a stream). This can leave bald spots and geode-style rings around each corner that are noticeable in the final piece. You can avoid this by slowing tilting your canvas until the 'body' of paint is right at the corner (and starting to go around it), and then tilt your canvas steeply towards that corner at the last second so that gravity carries it over and not just around it. As soon as that happens successfully, quickly correct the canvas back to level/the opposite corner to avoid losing too much paint over the adjoining edges. This is a hard technique to get right the first time, but you'll get a feel for how to do it – at first most people don't leave the canvas tilting sharply enough the extra half second or full second it takes to let gravity carry it over correctly.

Once that first corner is done, tilt your canvas back toward the center/opposite corner. You'll learn to see the thick bubble or 'body' of paint as it moves and slowly spreads over the canvas - look for ripples of movement where a section of the wet paint moves faster as you tilt. Once that main mass of paint reaches the rough center, tilt towards the corner to the left (counter-clockwise) of the first corner you started with. Repeat the slow tilt followed by the steep momentary corner-dip to cover this corner as well. Again bring your canvas back to level/slightly tilting away from the corner you just did to avoid paint loss over those edges. Moving counter-clockwise, slowly tilt your paint towards the next corner and cover it. Again, correct the canvas back to level, and do a slow tilt towards the last corner. You may find you have to angle the canvas towards that corner but also slightly towards center, so that you aren't losing all the remaining paint over that final edge as it moves. At this point, you may notice the paint is moving very slowly or not at all. If that is the case, use more paint in your next pour and practice your timing on the corner-dip technique to try to minimize paint loss.

Blotting Bald Spots on the Corners and Sides

Even the most experienced artists can have slightly bald corners or small bald spots along the edges of their work. One of the things that visually sets acrylic pour paintings apart is that the artwork continues cleanly right over the edges, giving the pieces a slightly 3D effect. I often employ the finger roll technique to get a clean cover to a bald spot without it looking muddy, instead of dabbing fresh paint there that may look odd. For the edges: Take the clean tip of your pointer finger and lay it in the bald spot, parallel to the corner. Gently roll your finger towards the nearest paint, then gently roll it back. The paint will stretch to follow your finger, covering the spot in a way that isn't at all obvious as it dries. For the top of the canvas, if your paint didn't quite reach the edge, you can use the same technique. Lay your finger along the edge, parallel to it, and gently roll it towards the paint, just barely touching it. Slowly roll your finger back – you should see the paint pulled along - and then gently scrape your finger down to pull that paint over the edge and cover the spot. Making sure your edges look clean and free of spots can add a lot of bonus points towards how professional your finished product looks.

2) The Fantastic Flip & Drag

This one is a personal favorite of mine, and starts out identically to the Flip Cup:

Part 1: Pick up your canvas (as much from underneath as possible so you hands don't take the wet paint off any more of the edge than necessary.) Pick up your cup in the other hand (but be careful not to squeeze it). This part will take some practice, but in one smooth motion, quickly turn the canvas almost fully upside down, and then lift your cup and set the canvas on top of it, as centered as possible. With the canvas is now laying on top of the cup, move your canvas-holding hand to the underside of the canvas itself – palm flat against where the cup is. Maintain pressure from both sides as you flip the canvas back over, keeping the cup firmly attached (and the paint trapped inside until you're ready, but do NOT squeeze your cup!) Once you're holding the canvas flat again with the cup upside down on top of it, you can gently let go of the cup (which should stick due to suction). Use both hands on either side to very gently set the canvas back down flat on your work surface.

Here is where this technique varies!

Part 2: Position your cup towards the farther end of your surface (about 2/3rds of the way down the canvas from you) by very gently dragging the cup (as you gently push down to maintain suction). Tap the top of your cup a few times to encourage all the paint to pool at the bottom (which helps avoid drips) and wait a few moments for everything to slide down. This time when you squeeze and gently lift, you need to carefully maintain very little distance from the canvas to the bottom of the cup (approximately 1/16" inch) as you slowly pull the cup towards you. As it gurgles out some artists will get flustered and pull the cup away or set it back down again. Try to stay steady as you pull it towards you and paint pools out from under the sides and behind it. This creates a 'sweep' of color across the top from the edges of the cup dragging through the paint. This can add some really beautiful movement to a piece before stretching. It also more evenly distributes the paint across the surface, which means less tilting is needed, and thus less distortion of the lacing and cells.

3) Tube Pour

This pour is very similar to effect you get if you poke a hole in the bottom of your cup on a flip cup or flip and drag. You can reuse a cardboard tube from a paper towel roll (cut in half) or toilet paper roll (both are only good for one use). Instead of flipping your canvas over, you would wet prime, then set the roll end down into that wet paint and hold it there with one hand while you fill it with paint. You can do this 2 main ways:

1) Layer the colors directly in the tube as you would a cup. The downside to this one is that you will be working one-handed to fill it, and because of that drips are likely to happen. This is not the best option if you are trying to leave negative space (which this pour is great for). The upside is you can easily layer your tube with any of the techniques discussed above for layering cups.

2) Layer a cup, and then pour that cup directly into the tube until it is full. This will cause a lot of blending and soft gradiations, but if you are using oil in your pours this can result in some great cells.

You can treat the tube pour as either a flip cup or flip & drag, pulling it directly up or slowly releasing the paint as you drag it across the surface. There is a variation of the straight pull up that I am fond of doing - it involves either setting your tube down into a thick puddle of paint or putting it down and pouring paint around it. If you very gently lift the tube, your paint will pool out quickly under the color around the tube, which creates absolutely beautiful lacing as the colors rise and break the surface tension.

4) Dipping

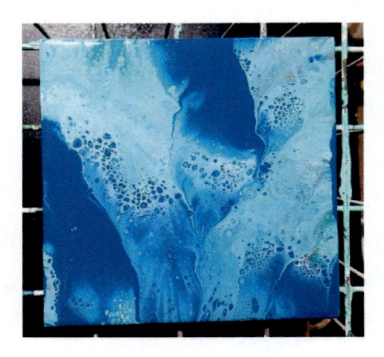

Dipped 4" Tile Coaster

You may notice after a few pours that there is quite a bit of wasted paint in the bottom of your tubs/work surface. One of the reasons I council using the same set of colors for several pieces each time you work is so that you can 'dip' pieces after you are done pouring! Whether it's a small canvas, tiles, wood pieces, or anything else that will fit, you can make gorgeous 'dipped' pieces with this leftover paint. Here are some tips for dipping:

1) If you use oil in your pours, you need to dip pieces in the freshly pooled paint immediately after a pour. The oil in the pour will quickly rise to the top. If you wait too long it will be the first thing your dipped object touches, leaving bald spots you cannot fix.

2) The trick to clean looking dips is two-fold: look for spots that have a lot of contrast (light/dark colors) and never hit the same spot twice (to avoid muddiness).

3) When you dip you'll find the most pleasing textures on square or rectangle pieces happen if you pull one corner up first, then pull the piece up diagonally across the center.

4) Immerse your piece totally to cover the edges. I often drop in 1" square tiles for magnets, pushing them down just a little to cover all the edges. I then pull them up by squeezing 2 corners with the my thumb and forefinger, with one corner coming up first. Afterwards, just lay them flat on a drying rack and let them settle.

5) Blowing out airbubbles/torching for bubbles will probably be necessary, as you've pushed air into the paint during the dip.

6) You can do bigger pieces this way too, if your tub is large enough and flat in the bottom. You can also drizzle contrasting colors and metallic colors on top of the pooled paint to get a more interesting large dip. Experiment!

5) Ribbon Pours

Ribbon Pours are probably the most straight-forward of all

the pouring styles. Keeping your canvas flat, you tilt your cup and pour the paint out - the variation comes in how you do it! Keeping your cup low and in one spot to create a puddle or higher and moving side to side to create very defined lines - this is one to play with! The only real trick is making sure there is enough paint in the right places to cover your entire canvas when you stretch it - especially if you want to keep those lines clean for movement and directionality! Ribbon Pours are often the technique of choice for doing larger works.

6) Tree-Ring Pours

Tree-Ring pours are a tried and true crowd-pleaser, but they do take some technical skill and planning to pull off successfully. While in the planning stage, try to keep the following tips in mind:

1) A truly successful tree-ring pour has high color contrast, no muddiness, and an organic shape that hasn't been over-stretched. Use whatever paints you have with the best pigment content, and leave them a little thicker than you might in a normal pour - you want your colors to keep strong opacity.

2) While you're learning this technique, high contrast is the name of the game. Start simply, with colors that are on polar opposite ends of the colors scale. For example: black, white, bright red, turquoise. Layer your cups for optimal contrast, and layer thickly using the first layered cup example above. When you tilt your cup to pour, do it from 45 degrees from the point you added paint down the inside of the cup (If that point is South, pour the cup from Due East or Due West, not North.)

3) The hardest part is keeping the small circles you make very tight, to avoid messy looking rings. Imagine there is a penny on

your canvas, and you are aiming to pour directly on it's outside edge over and over in a circular motion. When the cup is nearly empty, stop the motion above the dead center, tilt your cup nearly vertically to get the last few drops, then tilt it quickly up and away to avoid drips.

4) Tilting is very important on this one. If you want a complete circle with a 'geode' type feel, stretch it in a circle from one corner to next with the smoothest movements you can, leaving some cohesive negative space. If you want something a little different, tilt your least favorite side off one corner. The more you stretch, the more the 'rings' will widen and gain texture!

Post-Pour Pointers

Clean Edges Example by Briana C.

1) Wipe the underside of each edge before you leave the pieces alone to set and begin to dry. Use the blade of your pointer finger, wipe as you go around each edge under your pieces until that edge is dry/slightly tacky, but no longer wet, cleaning your finger between each swipe. Leaving paint there to drip off will continue to pull paint over the edge of your piece, potentially causing run-off and a loss of that piece. Briana C. (@IndigoImpressions on IG) started the hashtag 'ShowMeYourEdges' to help teach people to pay attention to how their edges look and to get those under-edges clean before they set the pieces up to dry.

2) Double check for levelness. Nothing is more heartbreaking that coming back to check on freshly pouring pieces and seeing that your favorite one has lost a dramatic amount of paint over one side. The best way to eyeball your levelness is to come back 5-10 minutes after a piece has been set down and look for new drips on any of the edges underneath. If you cleaned the edge under your piece properly and you have new drips, your piece is higher on at least one side and needs to be corrected.

3) Blow/Torch The Last Air Bubbles. Depending on the thickness of your paints and your pours, air bubbles can take up to 15 minutes to surface on your piece. Popping those with either your breath or a torch can help avoid pitmarks and keep your surface smooth for glossing.

Utilizing Negative Space

Negative space is space within your artwork that remains a single, unrelieved color with a sweep of color/texture/shape that goes through/around it. Negative space gives your eyes somewhere to 'rest' when taking in a piece, but can also really accentuate the cleanliness, colors, directionality, and movement of a piece. Negative space is often white or black, but using bright colors is, in my opinion, underrated and under-utilized. Negative space can be planned into a piece from conception or added in later to make it more successful overall.

'Lupus Ribbon III' - 2018

    This piece was a tube pour with a layered cup poured directly into the tube, then dragged through a black paint that was used not only to wet prime the canvas but also poured around the base of the tube before the drag. The black accentuates the shades of purple, the pearlescent micro-pigments added to the colors, and the feminine shape suggested by the pour itself.

'Hurricane' 2018 - Tree-Ring Pour with Negative Space

This piece was a black-edged tree-ring pour on top of a very soft, monochromatic stretched pour. The blue and gold hurricane shape edged in black was successful, but the colors that had been pushed towards the outside of the canvas weren't working with it. I hand-painted those outer edges black to create negative space and draw the eye into the swirl of the tree-ring without being overly busy.

Consistency

The concept of consistency is one that professional artists know well! When I see an artist who has a very consistent look across their body of recent works, it tells me that they really understand their personal style, mediums, techniques, and their overall process. If you prefer to do something a little bit different every time you work, that is perfectly fine! I personally love to experiment with new ideas/techniques often, even though my pieces tend to have a similar style and texture. You may find that while experimenting you create something that is just stunningly beautiful, and is something that people really respond to and hopefully are eager to purchase. The question is, can you re-create it if asked? If you can reach a place with your work where you can consistently recreate that effect/style/technique in your work, you will be seen as a more professional artist - and a more sellable one. However, consistency can be a double edged sword. The upside is that finding consistency in your work is often seen as finding your 'voice' - that style that is recognizably 'you.' The downside is that many professional artists get stuck in a visual cookie-cutter, recreating piece after piece - all of them nearly identical because they are extremely sellable. A good example would be the beach-scene-from-above overload currently on Instagram. There are so many artists doing beach scenes (using acrylic pouring and resin) that it has all started to blend together into an overly generic look that can be really beautiful but is ultimately forgettable. If you love what other artists are doing, but find a way to make it your own!

Chapter 5: Finishing Work

Here are the basics you need to know to spray finish your pieces/ We will discuss other coating options later on.

1) Find a dust-free, well ventilated area for this, and wear a mask! It may test your patience, but you absolutely must wait for piece to dry completely. The canvas should not feel cool from underneath, even if the top layer looks dry. Wait 24 hours after you are completely sure it is dry before starting.

2) Lightly sand with your extra fine sandpaper, gently smoothing the surface and edges (until just a little dust is visible and you can't feel any major bumps or ridges), as well as any bumps on the under edges from paint drips. This makes for a nice, smooth, glossy surface. Gently wipe down with a lightly damp sponge or rag to get the dust off, then allow at least an hour to dry.

3) Apply your first coat of finishing spray, edges first, then a light coat on the top, moving your hand gently from side to side in a continuous motion, carrying the spray right off the edge of the canvas to avoid pooling at the edges. There should be no dull/satin looking spots after each layer, but especially after the second and third. Allow 2 hours to dry before applying the second coat. Turn the canvas 180 degrees so that you can hit the farther edges first (to make sure between the two coats that the edges were all evenly coated all the way around) and then again add a top coat. Approximately 4-6 hours later, your piece should be completely dry and not tacky to the touch. At this point, I usually add a third layer just to the top, around the outside edges first, using the same technique but moving slowly and allowing the spray to apply thickly. This results in a very thick glossy finish.

4) Try to allow at least 3 days before you move or pack your piece. Finished pieces may feel dry, but the gloss needs to fully dry and set, and is much less likely to be damaged in transit if it has plenty of time to breath after the last layer. I also do not suggest stacking finished pieces without something between them, as unset finishes can attach to each-other can cause damage to your work. Curing times can vary wildly, so the accepted standard is the longer piece can cure the better - ideally about a week.

Chapter 6: Going to the Next Level

Working Larger

Starting out small is a great way to hone your skills and gain technique and consistency, but eventually you will want to (or be asked to) work larger. Be confident in your style, your color choices, and your game plan before you get started. Doing a large piece can be daunting - not only in difficulty, but in the financial investment involved. Most people wait for consumers to request larger commissions before they attempt working larger, and that is perfectly fine! If people are going to invest a lot of money is something (artist or art buyer), they want a great result! My best advice is go into your piece with a plan and test your color palette on smaller pieces first, so you can refine it before you do the larger one. If I'm setting up for a big canvas or wood cutout, I mix my colors and additives, then pour on a smaller canvas in the same exact way I plan to pour on the bigger one. I may find I need one color darker, one color thicker, more oil here, more pigment there, etc. The best way to be prepared is to check and double check, and always remember your professional touches - clean corners, dry edges underneath, level surface, no air bubbles. Little details can make all the difference between 'nice' and 'professional' looking artwork.

Working on Non-Canvas Items

If you don't have easy access to affordable canvases, I highly suggest wooden cutouts like those offered at PrimalFlowPaint.com. Look for cutouts that are at least 1/8" thick to avoid bowing/curving as it dries! The caveat with working on anything wood is that you have to make sure you do your prep work and that your pour isn't applied too thickly. Any kind of wooden surface will absorb the moisture from the paint and cause cracking and crazing as the inside layer of paint dries faster than the outside layer due to absorption. Wood is more of an intermediate material to work on, but accessibility does come into play depending on your access to Arts & Crafts stores. Wood cutouts also lend the ability to do cute, funky, and highly sellable shapes. These pieces can be a lot of fun to do, but the technical skills needed are a bit higher. If you attempt intricately shaped flat pieces, the best advice I have is to dry prime AND wet prime, using a flat tool to make sure every single edge of the cutout has wet paint on it before you pour.

Flow Painted Vintage Violin, 2018

     Don't be afraid to get really creative with what you paint on! I personally rarely work on canvases, preferring instead to work on acoustic instruments, wood, vintage bowels, and tiles. People want to connect to what you're making, and what you paint on can bring personality and charm into your work before you ever add a drop of paint.

High End Paints & Additives

     One of the things that really sets acrylic pouring apart as an art form is how many different materials can be used! Acrylics, Oils, Inks, Pigments, Resins, Glitter, 3D Elements like tiles and crystals - the options are literally endless. However, high-end paint brands like Golden aren't always an affordable option - even for professional artists. That being said, being able to buy and successfully use a pure, vibrant, opaque pigment (for example,

Phthalocyanine Blue) can be a game changer in your work. Understanding the chemistry of every single pigment - how they react to each-other and to additives and mediums - can let you tightly control their reactions and set your work apart with a vibrancy and consistency that is unmatched. Artists like Briana C. (@IndigoImpressions) dive deeply into that chemistry and are extremely knowledgeable about it - and understandably have a clear preference for one brand over another because of it! We all have our comfort zones and understanding of the chemistry involved, but you can always learn more if you're willing to challenge yourself. I may not use the most expensive paints out there, but I can still talk at length about their pigment density, opacity, hydrophobic qualities, lightfastness, etc. because I have put in the time and really gotten to know my materials and how they work together.

Functional Art & Decor

Functional Art like coat hooks, furniture, instruments, etc. can be a terrific niche market, but can require some more advanced skills to do successfully. If your piece is going to be touched/moved/utilized frequently, a couple of coats of spray gloss probably won't work. You'll need to invest in something more durable, like glass or resin, to protect your artwork. If your piece will be in direct or even partial sunlight, your paints will need to be lightfast and your coating non-yellowing. Take all of these elements into consideration before you start, and price accordingly. Doing small tables is a common functional artwork choice, but make sure your piece will hold up in the long run!

Fun & Funky Moosehead Coathook

     Resin in a great option to add a beautiful glossy look to any piece, but it can be restrictively expensive and very technically challenging. Ordering small bottles to play with is great if you have the resources, but the best option for new artists is to build up some clientele and sales before you go all out with such an expensive medium. It also requires a great deal of research, as not all Resins and Epoxies are created equally or well-suited for artistic applications. A good resin coating will at least double what you need to charge for your work, and putting a resin coating on mediocre artwork won't magically make it a successfully execute piece of art. Focus on getting to the level you want to be at artistically - <u>then</u> kick it up a notch! I personally use Pro Marine Supplies Resin, but I've experimented with several brands.

Resin Sealed Functional Tea Tray

Building Your Brand

There are more tips than I could begin to put here to jump-start your Art Career (or even just refocus it with this new style!) I'm going to focus on the tips and tricks that have worked for me personally, but also that I can identify as dos and don'ts for a lot of Artists online.

1) Build Your Base! Friends and Family are the best place to start, because they will usually take an interest and support your dreams right out of the gate. What are friends and family for, after all? However, you can definitely fatigue your base with constant posts asking for financial help or trying to sell your work, so go about it strategically. If you have an Instagram and a Facebook, learn to recognize the differences in how you should post. You can put pictures of everything on Instagram - your followers there will quickly expand into a whole world of people with the same interests, aesthetics, and artistic goals. Instagram is a great place for the random posts - from process pictures and demo videos, art inspiration posts, and even failed pieces! You should be more selective about what you share from there to Facebook. Those posts are what you put in front of the audience that you probably know and know well, but may not be as interested in the artistic nitty-gritty. Share your best pictures and videos, but try to keep it to 1-2 posts a day. Being selective will help you gain an eye for what kind of pictures people really respond to.

2) Tone is Everything! Begging people to buy your art can be demeaning, but may also feel necessary - especially if your ability to keep creating new work is completely dependent on selling what you've already made. This is where being strategic comes into play! If you only put one or two posts in front of your main base each day, be sure to talk about how much you enjoyed making the piece, maybe what inspired you, and <u>always</u> include 'Available' or 'Sold.' It's always important to try to be conversational - talk *with* your viewers, not just *at* them. It's may be more important than you might think to share a 'Sold!' piece whenever you have one - herd mentality is real! If your artwork is desirable to others, it will become more desirable to people who may not have thought about buying it before seeing a few 'sold' posts.

'Sold' Post on Instagram by @WetPaintByWendy

3) Professionalism - The Achilles Heel! Sometimes you need to create an entirely separate mentality and social media identity for for 'You - The Artist' and 'You - The Person.' Facebook is a great place for snarky memes, political cartoons, and humorous (but often profanity-laden) videos, but all of these can hurt your image as a serious professional. If you need to create an entirely separate Instagram or a Facebook Business Page, do it! People may love your work but unfollow you (and thus never buy from you) because of a single post they perceive as immature, crude, petty, or political, or religious.

The second part of professionalism to address is picture and video quality! If you post a process video, chances are no one will ever see the end if you post a 1 minute video where the first 20 seconds are dead flat as you prepare to work off to the side. Taking bright, naturally lit pictures of most artwork is best, but can be tricky and require some ingenuity! Research photographing artwork or download video editing software if you need to - the resources out there are plentiful! I personally use a refurbished Galaxy s7phone for my photography and videos, but it works extremely well - especially if I'm mindful of lighting conditions more than anything else. The best lighting conditions possible are a cloudy day or a morning before the sun has gotten very high or bright! The light then is soft and diffused, but bright enough for the camera to pick up fine details. Taking pictures in direct sun, heavy shade, or artificial light usually won't render great results.

      There are a million more elements to being a successful flow artist, but not nearly enough pages available to jot them all down. Try to remember the Golden Rules of Artistry: Be Adaptable, Practice Makes Perfect, and Believe in Yourself! If you aim for every piece to be the best piece you've done thus far, you will always be learning and evolving because you are truly challenging yourself. Learn to take constructive criticism, but ignore anyone who would restrict your creativity or dampen your passion. If your passions are put into your work, people will naturally respond to it. On the other side of the coin, the world is very commercially driven. You may have to paint some generic-feeling commissions, but try to see that as a challenge too. How can you fit their expectations AND make that piece uniquely you?

In closing, to to remember that this art form isn't about control - it's about enjoying your journey and connecting with your artistic instincts. It's all about passion, experimentation, and balancing know-how with the ability to let go and just create!

Glossary

Palette: A Selection of Colors or a Color Scheme utilized in a piece of Art. A Monochromatic Palette would be comprised of colors that all touch each-other on a color wheel, such as all blues, or all reds & oranges.

Ratio: In reference to mixing paints to mediums & additives. 1 part paint to 2 part medium would be a 1:2 ratio; 1 part paint to 2 parts medium to 1 part dry pigment would be a 1:2:1 ratio. Keeping track of your ratios while you work and experiment will dramatically help you in finding what ratios you need to get certain effects, and help you gain consistency with your techniques.

Muddy: In reference to acrylic pouring, a noticeable effect earmarked by different colors over-blending and losing their vibrancy. The loss of distinction between colors and tones can make for a flat, monochromatic piece. Pieces can also appear 'Muddy' or 'Busy' when too many colors/textures/shapes are present and the piece has no clear focal point or movement to carry the eye through.

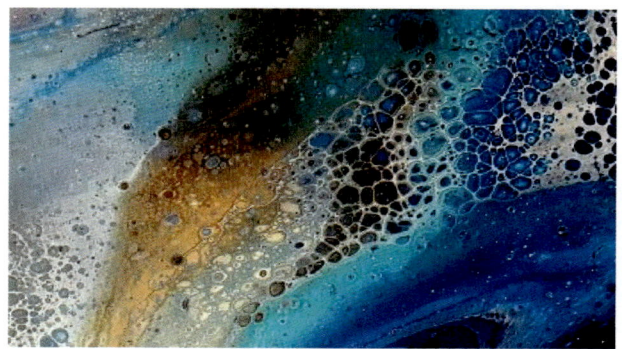

Lacing Example

Lacing: An effect that resembles antique crocheted lace doilies or water breaking on a beach. Lacing is often achieved by having very thin layers, or a very thin-water based color layered on a thicker color containing an oil additive. In Resin work, it is often achieved using air pressure at the right moment to spread a thin layer of one tinted color of Resin over another. There are many ways to achieve this effect, but creating it consistently can be challenging.

Body: In reference to stretching your artwork, the main mass of paint that tends to form a quickly spreading bubble when poured/released onto the canvas. Being able to recognize and control that 'body' can result in less loss of paint and optimal creation of movement/balance in a piece.

Contrast: In reference to tones, choosing colors that vary in how light/dark they are. Pieces that are to monochromatic in their tones tend to have much less visual interest to them than pieces that have at least one color that sharply varies from the others. For example, a pastel palette of pink, yellow, and light orange would benefit from a contrasting color like dark red, chocolate brown, or copper.

Surface Tension: Scientific Definition: 'the tension of the surface film of a liquid caused by the attraction of the particles in the surface layer by the bulk of the liquid.' In reference to acrylic pouring, purposefully planning for elements to break through the very top layer of paint in a pour; i.e. pigment particles, oils, and water particles rising through (and spreading) to create lacing and cells.

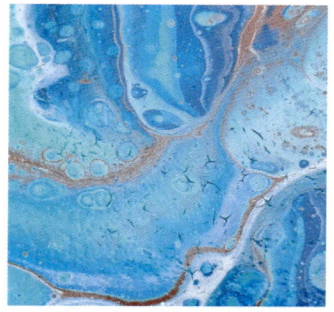

Crazing Example

Crazing: A defect which effects pieces primarily during the drying process. It can resemble small straight cuts, hairline fractures, or a patterning similar to a dry creek bed in the midwest. Crazing/Cracking can be caused by many issues, but primarily occurs when a piece dries too quickly - especially if the paint is too thick. Trial and error with mediums and techniques is the best way to avoid this issue.

I would like to say a BIG thank you to the Artists who agreed to contribute their pictures to be featured in this book!

Find them on Instagram:

Wendy MacDougall, British Columbia, @WetPaintByWendy

Briana Coleman, DC Metro, @IndigoImpressions

~~~

About the Author

Kegan Kidd is a Flow Artist from Deep East Texas. He graduated with a BFA from Southern Arkansas University in 2011. He discovered Acrylic Pouring after developing Rheumatoid Arthritis in his hands, limiting his ability to sculpt or use a paintbrush. He developed the first Internationally Available line of Pre-Mixed Acrylic Pouring Paints to help make this technique more accessible all over the world - largely because he strongly believes in it's therapeutic benefits.

Find Primal Flow Studio Artwork and Primal Flow Paint Here:

www.Facebook.com/PrimalFlowStudio
www.Instagram.com/PrimalFlowPaint
www.PrimalFlowPaint.com

Find Instructional and Demo Videos on Youtube @PrimalFlowPaint

Made in the USA
Middletown, DE
30 December 2018